Flies

Michael Dickman *Flies*

COPPER CANYON PRESS
PORT TOWNSEND, WASHINGTON

Cover art: Jean-Michel Basquiat, *Untitled*, 1982. Oil paint stick and
graphite on heavy white rag board, 60 x 40 inches.
Princeton University Art Museum, lent by the Schorr Family
Collection.

Copper Canyon Press is in residence at Fort Worden State Park in
Port Townsend, Washington, under the auspices of Centrum. Centrum
is a gathering place for artists and creative thinkers from around the
world, students of all ages and backgrounds, and audiences seeking
extraordinary cultural enrichment.

LIBRARY OF CONGRESS CATALOGING-IN-PUBLICATION DATA
Dickman, Michael, 1975–
  Flies / Michael Dickman.
        p. cm.
ISBN 978-1-55659-377-2 (pbk. : alk. paper)
1. Title.

PS3604.I299F55 2011
811'.6—dc22

98765432 FIRST PRINTING

COPPER CANYON PRESS
Post Office Box 271
Port Townsend, Washington 98368
www.coppercanyonpress.org

Acknowledgments

Grateful acknowledgment is due the editors of the following magazines, in which these poems first appeared: *The American Poetry Review, Critical Quarterly* (UK), *Field, Narrative, The New Republic, The New Yorker, Ploughshares* and *Tin House.*

Thanks to the Lewis Center for the Arts at Princeton University for a 2009–2010 Hodder Fellowship. I am happily indebted to Paul Muldoon, C.K. Williams, and Susan Wheeler for their support.

Thanks to the Lannan Foundation for the gift of a residency in Marfa, Texas.

I wish to thank my friends, family, Michael Wiegers, and Copper Canyon Press.

Many of the poems in this book were written in memory of my older brother, Darin Hull.

for Phoebe

Contents

Flies

Dead Brother Superhero

You don't have to be
afraid

anymore

His super-outfit is made from handfuls of oil and garbage blood and
      pinned together by stars

Flying
around the room
like a

mosquito

Drinking all the blood
or whatever we
have

to save us
who

need to be saved

•

I whispered   *To the rescue*
and sat
on the dead edge
of my bed
all night
and

all morning

My feet did not touch the floor

My heart raced

I counted my breath like small white sheep and pinned my eyes
        open and stared at the door

Any second now
Any second
now

•

He saved my brain
from its burning
building

He stopped and started the bullet in my heart
with his teeth

Just like that

He looked down from outer space through all the clouds birds
        dropping like weights

He looked out
from the center of the earth
through the fire
he was

becoming

in the doorway
and closed his eyes
his cape sweeping
the floor

Be More Beautiful

Whatever it is I was made for I haven't yet started

The morning makes its way up the street as a loose pack of wild dogs

Their invisible metal teeth

welcoming all the birds in the neighborhood

and me

The stars are wrong

Begin begin

I was just whispering

into my glass

pillow

•

Look it's nighttime again

I've been standing in front of a mirror for a hundred years

My glass clothes tossed across the bed

Trying things on trying things off

There just there

That's as far as I can go

Singing the one song I made up the only thing I have memorized—

You're a dog

You're a fucking

dog

·

My body is a dream of meat

It stinks and

sings

I dress it carefully and stick new Band-Aids on and take it outside so
    it can see and be in love

I hang it up on a hook

on a moon

to turn in slow circles

Open all night

Are you open all night?

I'm open all night

•

My face is wrapped tighter than anyone's face

Spray-painted on

Five holes

All smiles

If I was made to wake up and walk around and wave my arms
    beneath the trees then I'm doing it

My head pointed up my eyes full of leaves

Only yesterday

I wanted to be made out of nothing but your voice

and be more beautiful

and I was made

The Sea

for Franz Wright
and Denis Johnson

Everyone's first memory

First blue breath
first bath

Your loved ones swim out and back all morning tirelessly calling
     your name

All your enemies
drowned

Prospero helps the dead Neruda over the weird dunes
covered with bees
and scrub grass

gingerly stepping

around

the hypodermics in the jellyfish

•

My mother floats across the floor of our kitchen and kisses me on
    the forehead

My second memory
second
sea

Smoking a cigarette

She's alive
but she's acting
like she's
dead

That watery light people get sometimes
when they're first arriving
and when
they're

leaving for good

The cigarette ash falling
into the sink
it

sounds like the sea

•

The foghorns
are spelling someone's
name

Not your name

Maybe they used to
but not any-
more

It serves us right to be alive

We move out across the water in our stupid bodies and blow out the
     breakers one by one

Delivered

from our names
into some secret
home

Shaving Your Father's Face

First I get a father
from some city
of fathers

One with a neck

bright
red

And with all the bird bones in my fingers carefully tip his chin back
    into the light like love
     so I can see
     so I can smell

I tell a dirty joke and drag the steel across the universe

There's nothing better
than shaving your father's face
except maybe
shaving

your mother's legs

My bedside manner is impeccable

The white foam stays white

•

In the evening
his face attracts moths and
daughters

It's as if his chin is made of Christmas lights you have to shave the
    dust and family off it takes forever

I like to use Merkur Super
platinum-coated
stainless
steel

You can write on water with it

Rust free
Rostfrei

Made in Germany
so it will

last and last

·

Shaving my father's face
I'm not shaving
my face

I'm shaving my brain

Lifting
the gray folds
to get at the pink
parts

Stuffing toilet paper into all the new holes I cut so it looks like a
        field of red flags
        paper tulips
        love notes

The universe wants a close shave
It wants its hair
high
and tight

You could bounce a dime off Dad's skin

My hand
on your face can you
feel it

False Start

At the end of one of the billion light-years of loneliness

My mother sits on the floor of her new kitchen carefully feeding the flies
     from her fingertips

All the lights in the house are on so it must be summer

Wings the color of her nail polish

I like to sit on the floor next to her and tell her what a good job she's
     doing

You're doing such a good job Mom

She's very patient with the ones who refuse to swallow

She hums a little song and shoves the food in

They still have all their wings

It takes a long time because no one is hungry

·

At the end of one of the billion light-years of loneliness

My father trains the flies to walk from one end of his fingers to the other

One fly for every finger

It's going to make him rich

Their brains the color of his brain

All the nerves in your hands getting stepped on at once is very calming

Like being a pine tree

Next he's going to train them to walk across his eyelids

How to hide in the holes in his teeth

When he sings and he never sings we will see wings and brains

•

At the end of one of the billion light-years of loneliness

I stuff my mom and dad into a little red wagon and drag them out into the ocean

Waves the color of their eyelids

Beach glass

I swim alongside and tell them how good they look

Washed in salt

They haven't seen each other in a very long time so I wait awhile before hauling them back

Hauling them out of the underworld

The overworld

Dragging them out of their mansions of snow

•

At the end of one of the billion light-years of loneliness

My brother swims out into the ocean with his daughter holding hands
    and talking quietly

Flies drop into the water

His daughter was a fly for a while

Small and black and gleaming in the palm of his hand

He blew on her gently and she woke up

Some miracle

He swam out across the waves swinging her screaming above his head
    and looked just like a father

The new daughter

Her new father

•

At the end of one of the billion light-years of loneliness

My brother and I set sail in a red boat

He is almost old and tired so I do most of the rowing

The gods in their mansions are boarding up the windows

Time to move to a different neighborhood

We hold hands in the middle of the ocean and look just like a painting

His paint has just now started to chip away

He needs to be restored

Carefully, now

My brother

Emily Dickinson to the Rescue

Standing in her house today all I could think of was whether she
      took a shit every morning

or ever fucked anybody
or ever fucked
herself

God's poet
singing herself to sleep

You want these sorts of things for people

Bodies and
the earth
and

the earth inside

Instead of white
nightgowns and terrifying
letters

•

Here she comes
her hands out in front of her
like a child flying
above its bed

Her ankles and wrists held tightly between the fingers of a brightly
        lit parent home from a party

Flying

Her spine
flying

Singing   "Here I come!"

Her legs pumping
her heart
out

•

Heaven is everywhere
but there's still
the world

The world is Cancer House Fires and Brain Death here in America

But I love the world

Emily Dickinson
to the rescue

I used to think we were bread
gentle work and water
We're not

But we're still beautiful

Killing each other as much as we can
beneath the
pines

The pines
that are somebody's
masterpiece

From the Lives of My Friends

What are the birds called
in that neighborhood
The dogs

There were dogs flying
from branch to
branch

My friends and I climbed up the telephone poles to sit on the power
    lines dressed like crows

Their voices sounded like lemons

They were a smooth sheet
They grew

black feathers

Not frightening at all
but beautiful shiny and
full of promise

What kind of light

is that?

•

The lives of my friends spend all of their time dying and coming
    back and dying and coming back

They take a break in summer
to mow the piss
yellow lawns blazing
front and
back

There is no break in winter

I fell in love with the sisters of my friends
All that yellow hair!
Their arms
blazing

They lick their fingers
to wipe my face
clean

of everything

And I am glad
I am glad
I am
so glad

•

We will all be shipped away
in an icebox
with the one word   OYSTERS
painted on the outside

Left alone for once

None of my friends wrote novels or plays from the lives of my
          friends came their lives

Here's what we did
we played in the yard outside
after dinner

and then
we were shipped away

That was fast—

stuffed
with

lemons

Imaginary Playground

The swing sets
aren't really
there

Snow begins to pile up in the kingdom behind us

Everything here is metal and barkdust and sunlight and laid out on
    a white tablecloth for us to eat

If we want to eat it

One side of the teeter-totter is singing into the grass

That's the way to do it
put your face in the dirt
and belt it out

I'm hungry

I put my face in the dirt and sing

I pick up my knife

I pick up my fork

•

My friends are here
but they're difficult
to see

Come out come out won't work

They wear starry crowns
They imitate falling
leaves

I used to be
a tree

just like you

Burning needles all afternoon

I will see them again in their lives or out of their lives in the trees or
  out of the trees dressed like children

On the blacktop
we lie down in each other's arms
and outline our bodies
in chalk

•

Pine trees
the color of
a blizzard

There are no hiding places anymore

The merry-go-round begins to turn slowly all by itself what do you
      think about that?

I brought a picnic
and sat down in the barkdust
and looked out
over the

diamond

One friend comes limping over

One friend at a time
is all I can take
Look

someone wrote THE KINGS ARE RETURNING in the newly
      poured concrete right before it dried and they returned

All Saints

I made the mask
from scratch
also the wings
all by myself
in the shape of a sick child
or newly cut
grass

It was hard to stand up at first because the wings were so heavy but
I'm getting more and more used to them

More and more ready

Dripping
waves of silver paint
they shine like
the blind

But the beak is real

A real beak

instead of a mouth

•

I brought the new
body to school
wrapped in tinfoil
but left it in the coat closet
in a backpack with
my brain

It was dark in there and scary and there were woods that no one had
    ever mentioned before and probably
      never will again

I was called on all the time
despite staring out the window
as if the playground were
on fire

Stand closer

No one cared

Stand closer

The flames licked the blades

•

We will hold hands like children and sit on the floor in a large circle
        with our legs crossed in the late style of
        deathlessness

Waiting for
satori

What I wanted to show you
has disappeared
through a hole
in the back of my
head

What I wanted to tell you

If you pee your pants on the floor
you still have to sit there
on the spot where
you peed

A halo

seeping into the rug

Barnett Newman: Black Fire I

What I want more than anything is to get down on paper what all the
    shining looks like

All black all the time

Black petals black leaves
black pulse

I like to sit in the corner
and watch the light disappear
with both my eyes

God doesn't have any eyes

Hurricanes
Cottonmouths
Lakes

The list goes on and on

Shit gnats and
sunlight

but no eyes

•

The shivering
through the maple leaves
is something I can't stop
talking about

I used to ride a slick black tricycle beneath the trees but now I just walk

Or lie down
and stare up at nothing
or lie down and
stare up
at nothing

The underside of the leaves
covered in

ants

My nightlight

•

The black pedals
on my black
tricycle

look like wings

I put my feet on the wings and fly around the yard avoiding dogs and
      worms

The stars are
in the ground
with my grandfather
smoking cigars
and shining their
asses off

Grandpa has to hunch over
to fit under there
beneath the streetlights and maple leaves
beneath the stars
worms

The light comes up through his teeth

and

the black grass

Stations

I

The cactus flowers fold themselves into white paper swans the color
    of disappearing

Clean needles

You have to listen carefully like dirt

You have to fold back their wings with your wings

Dig yourself out with your fingers

Your teeth

You're going to die anyway and not because it's natural but because
    they want you to

They hand you your death they say here it is

A bag of piano keys

The little cross is somewhere in my room not doing imitations of
    birds

Not digging itself out

Even though it has four points

And can fly

II

I want to see your face again turn towards me your mouth

That's one thing

The other is your hands I want both of your hands inside me
    swimming around like fish

My heart makes all the light there is crawl across the floor and begs

The light panting the light rolling over

The light in your face sitting back on its heels wagging its tail and
    barking

Doesn't that feel good?

There will be no pain but it will still be hard to carry

There will be a lot of pain but you will still have to carry it

Your fingers swim from one hole to the next shedding small golden
    scales

The light heels and pants

The fish scatter

Doesn't that feel good?

III

The little cross is made out of something we can't see and we are
    made out of something the little cross can't see

Veins and skin reflected by more veins and skin can the little cross
    see that?

We invented a chimney let's feed it lambs

Feed it hooves

Holly

Choke it down

Leave piles of ash wherever we walk

The little cross is made out of every moving tree

Every singing limb

Every leaf

The ash behind me starts to drift off like snow in summer

There is a song we've been waiting for

There is a voice

IV

You will meet once again in perfection your mother on the street
    but you will not recognize her

Cusping her face with the palm of your hand

Sometimes   *I want you to fuck my face* is as close to tenderness
    as we can manage

Thank god you're not my mother

You're not my mother

From moment to moment God is the one pressing us against the
    glorious metal shining everywhere in the universe

Except when from moment to moment we are

I want you to do it like this

Like this?

Yes like this

Your new Boss is a Motherfucker

Her Masterblack Pants

Her Fat Fingers

V

What does the little cross want with us anyway?

To grind us into diamonds

To make us dance

To tear our arms off and throw them out into the yard like sticks

I need help carrying these sticks

The diamonds

Dancing

The little cross hunches in the corner and stares and drools
      coughing up white petals

It never takes its hundred eyes off us

When we feint to the left the little cross feints to the left

To the right to the right

When we call to our mothers

The little cross answers

VI

I want to watch you open your mouth again and keep opening

Stretching open the white world

You can put all ten of your fingers inside of my mouth if you want
      to later we can dry them off on your hair

I want to wipe off your face with my face

Drag my face across your body like a rag and wring you out onto
      the sheets

Your fingers will fit I promise

Your pinky ring

Once more with feeling

You can put your teeth inside my pillow

And stroke the keys

And float

Above the honey

Above the holes

VII

My mother is inside the little cross and my brother

Both my brothers and my sisters

What else is there

A long metal table where we all might sit down for a moment and eat

Hold knives

One by one they will want out

And the little cross will slowly get up and walk the vast hallway of
itself and clear away the dishes

When my brother fell down he stayed down

He will not get up again

Everyone wants to be let out of the little cross except for him

He's happy here

While everyone else is crying they are crying

To be let out

VIII

If you can hear me then you can crawl across the floor and save me

My heart is jumpy

My heart is a ball of red dirt rolling into the sea

Dirt and mercury

If you could meet anyone who would it be?

Your father alone in a nightclub inventing sadness in his wristwatch

The beginning of the world

The backup singers tonight are called the Daughters of Jerusalem

They shake it in the sea

The rest is fire

My heart bellies up to the bar and orders an unspeakable cocktail

I crawl across the floor in flames

The drinks are free

IX

The little cross curls up on my bed and growls

Sometimes it comes to this

Teeth in the air

And hair

All the dogs have been taught to fight and eat each other and not be
    scared and fuck death

They chase their own tails into the ground

Doing this

The little cross lifts its head for a moment before laying it back
    down heavy as the moon

A square jaw that's an anvil

It raises its anvils I raise my anvils

Snaps and shines

And sniffs the air

And barks

X

I want you to do it like this and you do it like this

My heart is a red ball of dirt balancing in the open sea where I left it
      in the toilet

Dog paddling

Fetching the stick and bringing the stick back

Happy almost all the time

Our bodies don't illuminate this room no matter how hard we work

My heart floats in piss

Your limbs sink in skin

My turn and then your turn and then my turn again

The water in the toilet boils

And boils over

God is the one

Except when we are

XI

Sometimes we are taken by the hand and sometimes we're not

On our hands and on our knees

This won't hurt a bit

I want to make it cry in the dark for its dinner

I want to make it sit up and sing

I lead the little cross around my room on a leash and make it lap up
    the mess it made

Chains pour around my feet

Then it's my turn

I sit up and sing

I lap up shit

I open my heart

I was a valuable nail in the lap of the lord

The collar the little cross brings me is nothing but light

XII

If you can hear me then you can save me

If you can hear me then you can crawl across the floor across the
    Milky Way

I believe in your body

I believe in hands and knees and trees

I believe in crawling across the floor

I believe in teeth and piano keys

I believe in needles

I believe in no wings

The tune they keep playing is the sound of flies eating sugar out of
    the palm of your hand

We enter the world listening to flies

We leave the world

We eat the sugar

We keep happening

XIII

I like to lie facedown in the little cross and pretend that I'm drowning

My hair floating in the drain

My blood pounding the roof of water

The little cross will save me from the undertow in the bathtub

It kills and saves and kills and saves and kills and saves and kills and saves

It uses the tip of a towel to dry the inside of my ear

Shaved clean

And returned to the shore to melt in the sun

I swabbed the deck

The world of shit

Is the world of shit

And yet

And yet

XIV

The little cross is so small that it can fit in the palm of my hand

It can fit in my brain

I didn't think there was room for it anymore on earth but there is room

The streetlights turn from red to red

The traffic stalls

The little cross is here and lies down in the grass the little cross is here
and lies down in the grass

From red to red

We are the loneliest murderers ever invented

I lie down in the grass

Hammered into love

You will not be able to mistake it

Like cancer in children

You will hear music

Flies

Then it's the flies
that wake me
up

It's the flies that gently get me out of bed and slip me into some
        clothes so I can walk around outside

In my body outside
in black and medicine green
in wings

I am tarred and feathered
and walk around
on their legs

all day

It's the flies that sweetly call my name

so I'll know it's time

walking all over my face
whispering and
eating shit

•

Put on your wings I put on my wings
Slide into your legs
I slide

into my legs

Medicine green
Cathedral green
Flying

stained-glass windows

My window wings smell like metal and my legs are very thin and
        can fly too you could thread a needle with them

Here we go
through the eye
of a needle

Through all the ten thousand eyes

Your mother's
Your brother's
Your sister's

•

It's my birthday again
for the last time
for a year
again

Thirty-three flies bring in a cake from the other room and set it on
        fire singing the song my name sings

Shoo-wop
shoo-
wop

No one's going to eat this cake

I don't even have any friends anymore

But the flies are my friends

Hold me up in the dark bar
where I drink black beer
pitcher after pitcher

Indian oceans for my birthday

of India ink

It's time to drag the family out
so I'll know I'm alive
and do

a little dance

My sister's eyes are green grass
My brother's are green-black

My mother's

The flies will have to life-flight me back home when I finish these
        encores and collect my flowers

I lost all my bets
on the living
and the dead-for-now

My brain wants out
it wants to roll around in the backyard
it wants to water the white
roses

•

I love it here
and am never going
to leave

The flies pull back the top sheet and warm up my side of the bed
        pushing my hair back out of my eyes
        with their long thumbs

They smell like light in childhood

Like trees

The flies behind my eyes start to drift off

They sound like static in the leaves

Ten thousand eyes
opening and closing
at once

There there   They begin to sing

The worst part is over

Gardening

I put my hands away

I take my hands
and put them in the dirt
for later

The endless maple leaves all pointing down toward the grass and
    the dead dogs

What's buried there is hair
and hearts

Then it's time to start

I dig up my hands so I can beat back the dogs

I beat them back into their hair
into their hearts
beating

one

after the

other

•

I dropped my eyes into a hole
into the earth
so I could see

Shovel shovel

Don't you want to lie down with your hands on your stomach
        rising and falling?

Let's all do the worm

From this position
I can see the fine hairlike
roots of the maple
begin
to begin

A lightning storm in the brain

In the green brainstem
of the wet
world

•

What do you think will receive us?

The front yard the backyard
fingers and
mouths

The calm green
breast of your
friend

There's nothing better in the world than belonging to the grass

I want to dig everything up
and beat back the dogs inside me
to make room for more dogs
more hearts
more hair

More teeth!

There's always some little thing
you've got to do

An Offering

Why not wrap the Lord up
in his sleeping bags
and put him downstairs
for the night

So he'll be quiet

The Lord your brother

Your friends
the Lord

The sleeping bags are covered in tiny cowboys and floating lassos
spinning and repeating out into nothing

The Lord nothing

Galloping
through
the house

The migraine he gives you is not a voice

Your voice isn't even
a voice

•

Why not wrap his voice up
in a white handkerchief
made of new silk
new worms
and tuck it away
inside your dinner
jacket?

Later you can use it for the offering when they ask us to empty our
        pockets onto the marble countertops

From now on I will be ready

My shoes will be the flat black surface of a lake

My hair will be moonlight

The first song I ever heard my mother the Lord

I wrap up her voice
and offer it to the white worms
working so hard
struggling
using their
teeth

·

I have made so many mistakes that I must wake all the Lords early
    so we can get a head start on cleaning some of this shit up

They roll out of their sleeping bags

They unravel
from the white star
in my pocket

My sister the Lord
My grandma and Lord
grandpa

My boss the Lord

I don't have anything else to give
but the loves of my life
their hands and feet
and look
they have
my
eyes

Ralph Eugene Meatyard: Untitled

Is the light supposed to do that?

I put on one scary mask after another and then hung them in the
    trees where they shined like giant floating jellyfish

Milk-filled condoms

Your mother's face

My brother is hanging from the branches

Hanging or swimming

Our T-shirts absolutely blaze

This is why we think God is white

I am shaken in the trees

I am smeared

•

In one wilderness my brother wears a plastic bag over his head and
    leaps from the barn door

In another there's nothing but leaves and needles

Light burns the water off the tips of ferns

It looks like a seizure

Sometimes we sit just inside the barn with no heads at all and hold
    each other

That's the best time

No heads at all

My arms around him

His arms

Around me

•

The children are trees

My brother waves from the branches with both hands

A seizure in the solid green air

Relentless resurrection

First I put on the mask that looks like my brother then I put on the
   other mask that looks like my brother

My older monster

The light is puking pure white onto the ground

It can't help it

First it cuts off your hand

Then it cuts off your arm at the elbow

Translations

My mother was led into the world
by her teeth

Pulled
like a bull
into the
heather

She only ever wanted to be a mother her whole life and nothing else
        not even a human being!

One body turned into
another body

Pulled by the golden voices of children

A bull
out of hell

Called out
her teeth out in front of her
her children
pulling

•

I walk my mother out
into the field
by a leash
by a lifetime
she walks me out
our coats
shimmering

I brush her hair

Wave the flies away from her eyes

They are my eyes

Who will ride my mother
when we aren't around
anymore?

Turned from one thing into another until you are a bull standing in
a field

The field
just beginning
to whistle us

•

I am led by the mouth
out into the
yellow

Light turning
to water in the early evening
the insects dying
in the cold and
returning
in the morning

I put on my horse-head

Led by a bit

A lead

My leader is tall and the hair on her forearms is gold

We lower our eyes
into the tall grass
and eat

The New Green

To wake up every morning in the pines in your bedroom and have to
     shake off the green nightlights is a blessing

I want to burn down the forest
that's been growing
all night
in my brain

I left a note in my brain in red Sharpie it says   *Don't forget the matches*

Embers go flying up to the top branches

The house
gets brighter and
brighter

Then I call down the hallway to my dead brother

Then more lights

•

In my home in my brain
I'm at home

The pine trees are beautiful and made of green needles the pine
        trees are beautiful and made of green needles

I went to sleep
and when I woke up
I was covered in
pitch

Nothing really happens to you when you're dreaming

Everyone alive is alive
everyone dead is
again

Through the new green
they come back
they can't

come back

but they come back

•

The lights inside the pines
are my pillow

I strike the matches on my teeth
and light the needles
I strike the matches
I keep being
alive

I didn't know that it would get easier but it does

The rain softly through the last of the branches is your voice

The lights are my pillow

My brother is my mattress

My mother turns off
the trees
and

tucks us in

Killing Flies

I sit down for dinner
with my brother
again

This is the last dream I ever want to have

Passing the forks
around the table passing
the knives

One thing I want to know is who's in the kitchen right now if it isn't me

It isn't me

The kitchen is full of flies
flies are doing all
the work

They light on the edge of the roasted chicken

The bone china

That's what they do

Light

●

I will look
more and more like him
until I'm older
than he is

Then he'll look more like me

if I was
lost

The flies need to be killed as soon as we're done eating this delicious
   meal they made

They serve us anything we want
in toxic tuxedos
and

shitwings

My brother and I wipe our mouths
scrape our chairs back from the table
and stand up

These are the last things we'll do together

Eat dinner

Kill flies

•

You have to lie down next to the bodies shining all in a row like
     black sequins stitching up the kitchen floor

It's hard to do
but you have to
do it

Quietly lie down and not sleep

We don't sleep

My brother and I work hard all night

Sticking their eyes
onto our earlobes and wrists
like Egyptian
jewelry

He is my emergency exit

I am
his

dinner date

Above Love

The cherry trees
wave to us from the shore
and take off their
clothes

They wave and wave

I took off my clothes and stripped down the bark into smooth red
    stems and took off your clothes

Along the beach
the red construction-paper foam folds
like a love letter
asleep in your jeans

I wave to you

The red foam unfolds and
you wave
back

•

Glass cherries
drop like mercury
into our mouths and
slide down
to the sea

You do not feel it and then you do

A sharp pain and then burning

It won't make you
pass out

The procedure is done with foam and rubber gloves and calls your
        name in the waiting room on the shore

I can tie the stem in my mouth
with my tongue
can you tie the stem
in your mouth
with your tongue

A perfect
red bow and
no hands

•

From stem to stem
we can walk beneath the cherries
above the red foam
above love
and live

Their glass stems shake quietly in the dark

Glass skins

What will we do when we don't have bodies anymore?

I want to hold you between my teeth

On the shore
we grow new skins
new glass
new skins

Between our teeth cherry blossoms

fall into the treeless

singing

Home

In heaven
ants are the doormen
to the flies

I climbed out of one butchered ballroom into another climbing out
      of my half-life into my new life on earth

My brother right behind me

Home

The ants are a straight line
showing us the way
out of here

The flies are a straight line
with wings

They live in shit

We lived in a little blue house with a maple tree in the front yard

One ballroom and then

another

•

I've always wanted my body
to work harder
at being
alive

The light you see in veins

Eyelids eye
lids

Snow

The wires in the leaves
their eyelids turning red blinking
on and off

My body won't do what I want it to it won't burn

It says   I hold your hands in snow

In my hands

I hold your face

•

What you want to remember
of the earth and
what you end up
remembering

The flies get stuck between the single-pane and the storm windows

Turning up the volume on everything

I could stay here for such a long time

And not go anywhere
not even with you
not even if you were
finally leaving

But your voice
there in front of me
where I am going
to live

About the Author

Michael Dickman was born and raised in Portland, Oregon.

Lannan Literary Selections

For two decades Lannan Foundation has supported the
publication and distribution of exceptional literary works.
Copper Canyon Press gratefully acknowledges their support.

LANNAN LITERARY SELECTIONS 2011

Michael Dickman, *Flies*

Laura Kasischke, *Space, in Chains*

Deborah Landau, *The Last Usable Hour*

Valzhyna Mort, *Collected Body*

Dean Young, *Fall Higher*

RECENT LANNAN LITERARY SELECTIONS
FROM COPPER CANYON PRESS

Stephen Dobyns, *Winter's Journey*

David Huerta, *Before Saying Any of the Great Words: Selected Poems*,
translated by Mark Schafer

Sarah Lindsay, *Twigs and Knucklebones*

Heather McHugh, *Upgraded to Serious*

W.S. Merwin, *Migration: New & Selected Poems*

Taha Muhammad Ali, *So What: New & Selected Poems, 1971–2005*,
translated by Peter Cole, Yahya Hijazi, and Gabriel Levin

Travis Nichols, *See Me Improving*

Lucia Perillo, *Inseminating the Elephant*

James Richardson, *By the Numbers*

Ruth Stone, *In the Next Galaxy*

John Taggart, *Is Music: Selected Poems*

Jean Valentine, *Break the Glass*

C.D. Wright, *One Big Self: An Investigation*

For a complete list of Lannan Literary Selections from
Copper Canyon Press, please visit Partners on our Web site:
www.coppercanyonpress.org

Since 1972, Copper Canyon Press has fostered the work of emerging, established, and world-renowned poets for an expanding audience. The Press thrives with the generous patronage of readers, writers, booksellers, librarians, teachers, students, and funders — everyone who shares the belief that poetry is vital to language and living.

Copper Canyon Press gratefully acknowledges board member

JIM WICKWIRE

for his many years of service to poetry and independent publishing.

MAJOR SUPPORT HAS BEEN PROVIDED BY:

Lannan

The Paul G. Allen Family Foundation

Amazon.com

Anonymous

Diana and Jay Broze

Beroz Ferrell & The Point, LLC

Golden Lasso, LLC

Gull Industries, Inc.
on behalf of William and Ruth True

Lannan Foundation

Rhoady and Jeanne Marie Lee

National Endowment for the Arts

Cynthia Lovelace Sears and Frank Buxton

Washington State Arts Commission

Charles and Barbara Wright

To learn more about underwriting
Copper Canyon Press titles, please call
360-385-4925 x103

NATIONAL
ENDOWMENT
FOR THE ARTS

WASHINGTON STATE
ARTS COMMISSION

The poems are set in Janson, revived by Herman Zapf in 1937 from the original old-style serif typeface named for Dutch punchcutter and printer Anton Janson. Book design and composition by Phil Kovacevich. Printed on archival-quality paper at McNaughton & Gunn, Inc.

The Chinese character for poetry is made up of two parts: "word" and "temple." It also serves as pressmark for Copper Canyon Press.